And Chaos Laughed

Helen Pferdehirt

BookLeaf Publishing

India | USA | UK

Presentation by *BookLeaf Publishing*

Web: www.bookleafpub.com

E-mail: info@bookleafpub.com

ISBN: 9789358735215

First edition 2023

*This book is dedicated to the people of
Mars, the Plutonians who became friends,
and Mr. Neil.*

ACKNOWLEDGEMENT

Thank you to the muses. May this be the start of a fruitful relationship.

PREFACE

Each poem in this collection is essentially a first draft. I had a lot of ideas about whether or not this collection should be themed, but the themes didn't play out. Instead each poem idea popped into my mind while doing other activities. I wrote the thoughts down and created the poems around each one.

You may not like them. I may not like them, but they now exist.

A Prayer to the Muses

Muses I call to you
Guide me
Sing through my soul
Paint these pages
With your inspiration
Fill my mind
With Orpheus' song
Help me build worlds
With words

Near Miss

Weight pressing into me
Warmth of touch
For the briefest of moments
my arms wrapped tight around the world
My heart
On the verge of stopping with anticipation never
relieved
A familiar feeling
One to be conjured up time and time again
The near miss so full I can see the path of what
could've been
Idyllic and unreal
A life that never was on this plane

The Girl in the Painting

She stares back at me with eyes that are full of
mischief and haunted by desire.
A moment of youth and beauty captured for
eternity.
A gorgeous mystery left behind.
The girl in painting, her life unknown.
I'm jealous of her and the secrets she keeps.
But those eyes,
her eyes,
burn green at the life she's forced to watch.

Another World

I can sometimes see
the glimmer of another world
existing just outside our own.
It calls to me
the other world
Inviting me in through my dreams.
I yearn to sleep,
to find the doorway opened.
Each time exploring something new.
Praying Morpheus will keep me under
just a little bit longer.
Each night I go a little deeper,
wondering if this will be the time
I refuse to come back.

And Chaos Laughed

We came to being in the void
Particles dancing to freeform jazz
No order
And Chaos laughed with delight

Then came the bonds
Connecting us to one another
Building worlds and bodies
And Chaos laughed with disbelief

Then those bodies sought further structure
Creating society and governance
and Chaos laughed with bitterness

Then rose the nonconformists
Longing to break free of the stifling order
and Chaos laughed with joy

Then came the freed soul
Returned to the void
No longer bound
And it laughed with Chaos.

Wrapped in Perfection

I am having a moment
where I am deeply so deeply moved by the
words of others
that I cannot develop my own
I want to organically write a line
that will echo in the minds of the ages
A line that moves others in ways that I have
been moved before
So wrapped up in the perfection of that line
that the story is never completed
One day it will be my characters
searching for an author
Causing hysteria and existential crisis

What Happens in the Shadows

Concealed in darkness
Wrapped in a cloak of night
The hidden parts lurking just out of view
The air stirs
Hair bristles
Focused mind listening for answers
But whose voice returns?
The universe? The long deceased? A diseased
mind?
What happens in the shadows is anybody's guess
when we don't know whose controlling us.

The Knight of Swords

I remember a time
when I so full of fear, yet brazen and bold.
A complex contradiction walking unknown
roads.
Decisiveness was easy,
strategy was hard.
I was the Knight of Swords.
Charging into battle with no thoughts but the
choice to win.
Now, the weight of my sword is a much greater
burden.
And yet, it is still in hand.
Waiting for the right moment to swing.

Spring

A heart beating fresh
With the dawn of a new day
Daffodils pushing up through the cold hard
ground
The world dressed in a cloak of Impressionist
pastel
Birds sing the song of life
Heralding relief at last

Apotheosis

That bit of ancient temple in her blood
Her general air of otherness
Woven from the very fabric of the universe
She is clad in dreams
Galaxies come to life in her eyes
She transcends all planes
The apotheosis of existence
She sees all

Fall

A familiar warmth
Floods the nostrils
The scent of prosperity and abundance
Lingers in the air
The world in a cloak of sunset
Whispers of endless possibility
Crackles in the fire

What Even is the Future

My body is already half embalmed
With very, very, dirty martinis.
Trying to glimpse beyond the veil.
Sometimes an out of focus mind sees
I hold the candle to the mirror hoping to Divine
the next 5 minutes
I can't even fathom tomorrow
As it drips I see pain headed towards me
Hot wax burns
I let it
A self fulfilled prophecy
"What even is the future?"
I ask the tarot cards
Wheel of Fortune every time

The Stories We Shared

I remember a cat on acid
You carried it in your hoodie pocket
Claiming to be pregnant with your nascent
homosexuality

I remember that trip to Moscow
A planned escape
The willowy woman and the dream of a different
tomorrow

I remember the charming sound of bullets
A kevlar wedding dress topped with Napoleon's
hat
And your existential dread

I remember the dragon's breath
A forgetful fog
The hero proven the fool

I remember weeping on the bow of a boat
Taking us to that fire tower
Awaiting a falcon to fly

I remember the stories we shared
At Blanche's Bar
Before you took your last flight

Hades

I've never understood why God's like Hades get
such a bad rap
It's not even he who does the death, nor does he
judge the soul
He just governs the land where our eternity is
met
Our human fears casting him in besmirched light

Winter

Old magic slumbers
Death lays in wait to take his place in the dance
of life
The world wrapped in a cloak of falling stars
cascading towards a beautiful end

Error

So many ideas lost
living their eternity on forgotten memory sticks
error 404 file not found
the mind still operating on Windows 97
Clippy begging to save the file
for one glimmering moment
the document might have been recovered
blue screens all the way down

Summer

The greener grass is painted
An illusion of fun under an oppressive heat
The world wrapped in a cloak made of the
promises of a gilded cage
With age comes the wisdom that you've been
lied to
The water level recedes
Bodies begin to pop up
Scattered for a million different reasons

A Manifestation

I understand
The color green
Freely given
Lovingly received
A cornucopia
Swollen to burst
Labor sewn
Bountiful harvest reaped

I understand
The color pink
Freely given
Lovingly received
Rose hip tea
A silver cord pulled taut
Two halves of a whole
Reunited

I understand
The color orange
Freely given
Lovingly received
Veins filled with pride
Radiating from the solar plexus
Confidence evoked
And so it is